FROM TRIENT PRESS

Jennie Arnold

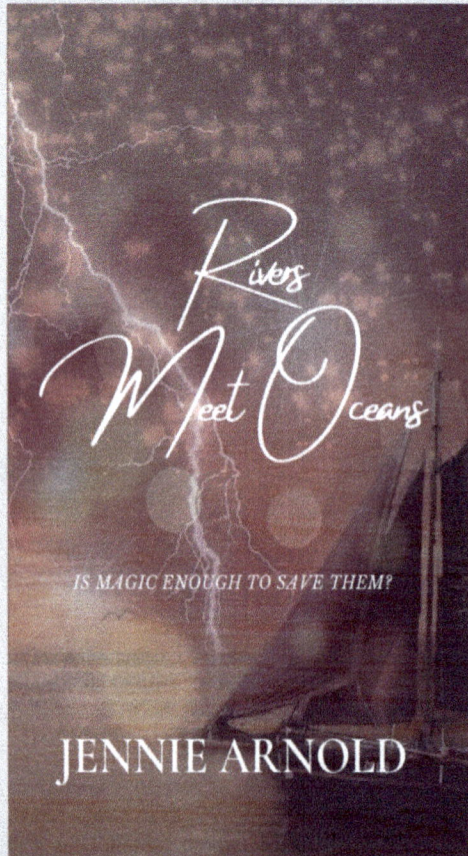

Rivers Meet Oceans

IS MAGIC ENOUGH TO SAVE THEM?

JENNIE ARNOLD

Trient Press

TRIENTREPRENEUR

ISSUE 5

CAPITAL SCHOOL

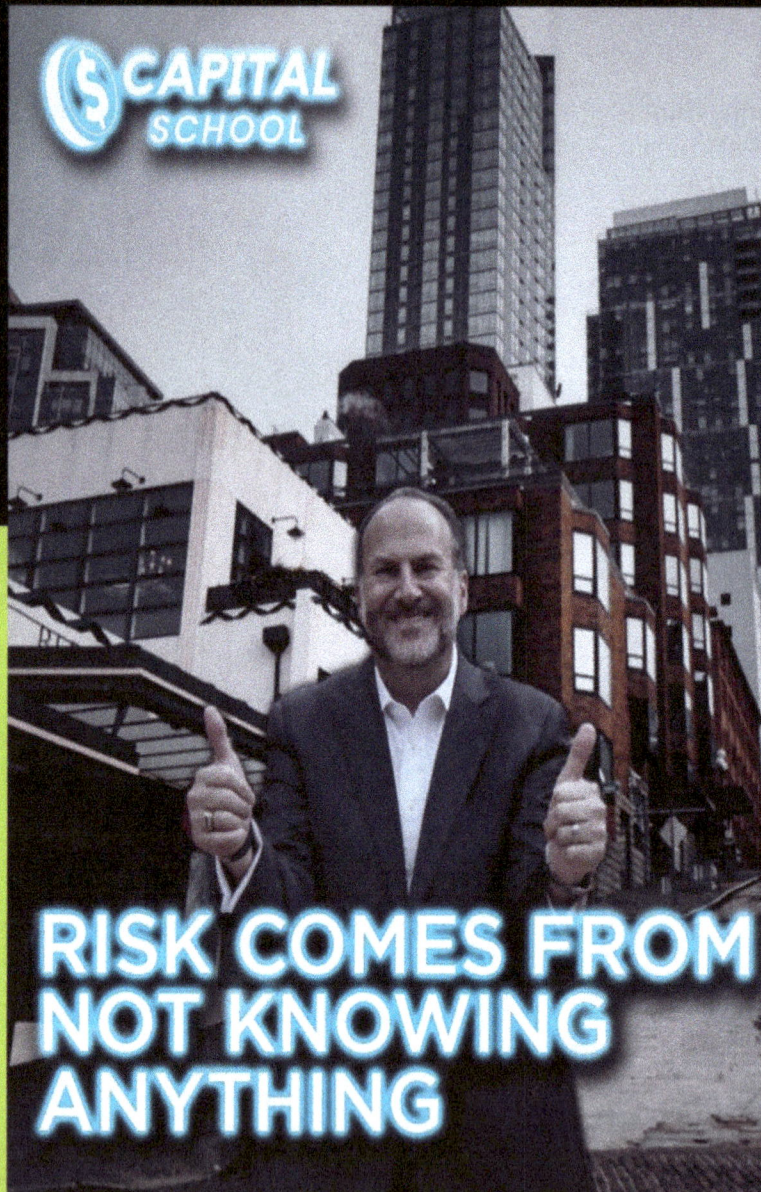

RISK COMES FROM NOT KNOWING ANYTHING

TODAY, CAPITAL SCHOOL IS ONE OF THE FASTEST GROWING COMMUNITIES OF ENTREPRENEURS, BUSINESS OWNERS, CEOS AND OTHERS LEARNING HOW TO ATTRACT, RAISE, AND CLOSE HNW INVESTOR CAPITAL. IT DOESN'T MATTER WHETHER YOU'RE NEW TO RAISING MONEY OR HAVE BEEN DOING IT FOR AWHILE - CAPITAL SCHOOL CAN HELP YOU GET TO THE NEXT LEVEL.

WHAT'S INCLUDED IN CAPITAL SCHOOL:

GET ACCESS TO MY FREE TRAINING
- HOW TO ATTRACT INVESTOR CAPITAL
- FOUR STEP BLUEPRINT TO RAISING CAPITAL
- SECURITIES LAWS | REGULATIONS
- CROWDFUNDING 101
- ACCESSING HNW LISTS
- GETTING INTO FAMILY OFFICES AND B/DS
- PLATFORMS FOR CAPITAL
- LINKS TO FAMILY OFFICE NETWORKS
- PUTTING YOUR "PITCH DECK AND OFFERING MATERIALS TOGETHER"
- AND MORE

AUGUST AUTHOR TIPS

Advice from Trient Authors

- Write what you want to read
- Write with intention
- Use psychology when writing
- Write as often as you can
- Eliminate distractions
- Research storytelling and story structure
- Always get feedback for writing
- Focus on new ways to phrase common visuals
- Practice writing when you're not writing
- Use strong language
- Just write to write
- Market your book as you would market your business

4 WAYS
Entrepreneurs Can Improve Their Time Management Skills

PRL

Managing time has become an all too real struggle for entrepreneurs these days. With so much to do in both their work and personal lives, it can be challenging to get things done in during a day. There are many ways for entrepreneurs to improve their time management skills to help them get more accomplished in less time. Here are four ideas for entrepreneurs to enhance their time management.

MAKE A SCHEDULE AND STICK TO IT

You can start to improve your time management skills by taking the time to organize your days and weeks in advance. While there will always be surprises that you'll have to deal with, youÕre more likely to be able to tackle those surprises better because you have an idea about what tasks and responsibilities you have to deal with each day.

PRIORITIZE

Learning how to prioritize is the second way to improve time management skills. If you want to execute your projects efficiently, then you have to decide which stages or components of the project are essential to your business. You have to be able to determine which activities and tasks will deliver the best returns for your business.

SET BOUNDARIES

If you want to be able to work in peace, then you need to inform those you work with when you're not available. Your partners and employees can't read minds, so it is your job to set appropriate boundaries when necessary. Make sure that you communicate your limits in a polite, yet direct manner to ensure that you can have the time you need to work on essential tasks.

ACCOUNT FOR GOOD DISTRACTIONS

There will always be distractions that get the best of you, no matter how hard you try to avoid them. However, no one can work for hours on end, and to stay productive, we all need breaks. The best thing you can do is accept this reality and try to incorporate some distractions into your schedule. Try to block out some downtime every day. This might mean setting aside a few minutes to take a short walk, grab a cup of coffee, or find some other stress management activities that you can do.

Managing your time requires discipline, planning, and a healthy attitude. However, if you get it right, you will start to notice improved productivity and lower levels of stress.

UNDERSTANDING THE LAW OF ATTRACTION

The law of attraction was first popularized in the 2006 movie "The Secret" by Esther and Jerry Hicks. It has had a huge impact on the mass consciousness, but there is still a large amount of confusion on its general application.

#1 - It's About Vibration, Not Thoughts

The main idea behind the law of attraction is that people manifest their reality not through their thoughts but through their vibration. The universe will respond to the energy generated by a particular thought as opposed to the thought itself. So you need to first get yourself into a good mood somehow before you will be able to manifest the energy of what you really want. After a while, the vibration becomes the reward, and the material items just appear after the fact.

#2 - Letting Go of Resistance

The level of internal resistance people have to the things that they want is not understood. People can have certain problems or issues, and then they create an identity of themselves out of these problems. When something comes along that is at odds with our idea of ourselves as inferior in some way, we resist. This can be observed when people win the lottery and wind up homeless 10 years later.

" THE VIBRATIONS OF THE THOUGHT IS WHAT ATTRACTS WHAT WE ARE MANIFESTING

We have to be a vibrational match to a new reality and not be attached to our former convictions. Otherwise, nothing will change. Many people are resistant to the idea of the law of attraction and will refuse to believe existence could be so simple. They will then continue to struggle believing that it is just how life is.

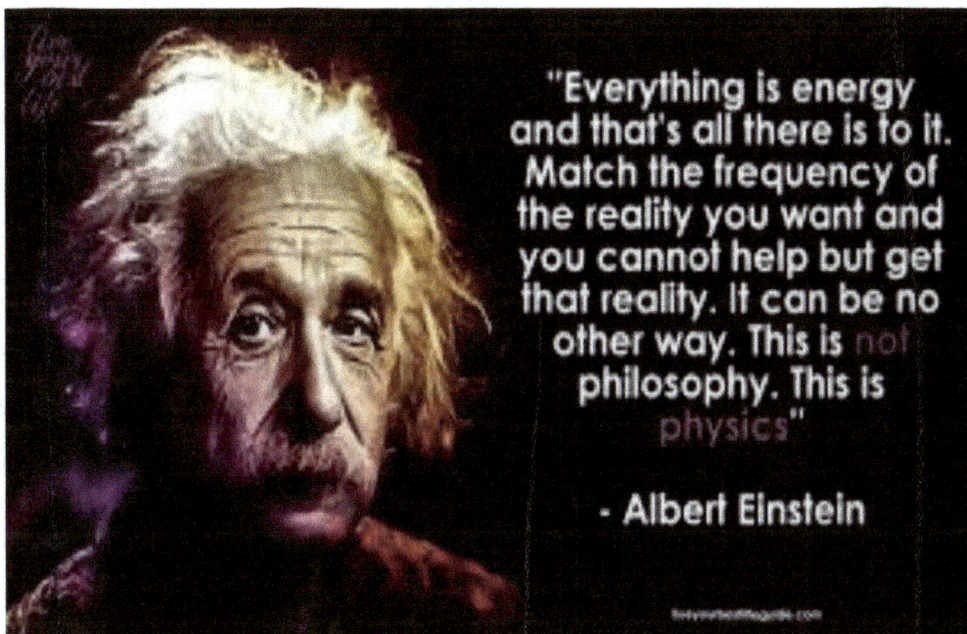

"Everything is energy and that's all there is to it. Match the frequency of the reality you want and you cannot help but get that reality. It can be no other way. This is not philosophy. This is physics"

- Albert Einstein

#3 - Don't Get Precise

It is important to understand the vibrational equivalent of what you want. You can have an image or a feeling about what you want that makes you feel good. But as you get more precise about how it is supposed to manifest, the universe has fewer ways that it can give it to you. There are millions of ways to get rich. But you can only possibly contemplate one or two methods which would involve years of work and labor. Consider that every successful person has vastly changed their business models. And they do so regularly. They might have a general idea about where they want to go, but they definitely innovate and change as these opportunities present themselves. So get happy and positive about the future, but don't get too precise about how it will materialize.

Ietef "DJ Cavem" Vita, a vegan rapper in the metro Denver area, encourages people of color to eat healthier by growing their own vegetables. He sells his own line of kale, beets and arugula seeds. (RACHEL WOOLF FOR KHN)

Seed Money: Black Entrepreneurs Hope Pandemic Gardening Boom Will Grow Healthier Eating

By Chandra Thomas Whitfield||MAY 20, 2021| Reprinted with Permission

DENVER — Ietef Vita had planned to spend most of 2020 on the road, promoting "Biomimicz," the album the rapper had released on his #plantbasedrecords label in January. Vita, known to his fans as "DJ Cavem Moetavation" and "Chef Ietef," had those plans unexpectedly cut short.

"We were in Berkeley, California, on Feb. 29, playing there and literally got out of town right before they shut the whole country down," recalled Vita, 34, who has performed for the Obamas and is widely considered the father of what's known as eco-hip-hop. "It was scary."

Suddenly sidelined at his metro Denver home with his wife, Alkemia Earth, a plant-based-lifestyle coach, and three daughters, Vita struggled to pivot. Eventually, he accepted that he would need to stay put and, as the saying goes, bloom where he was planted.

With his wife's help, he launched an impromptu campaign: mailing out thousands of the more than 42,000 packets of kale, beet and arugula seeds he'd planned to sell at his shows, all emblazoned with his likeness and the QR code to hear his digital album. With the help of a crowdfunding campaign, he sent them at no cost to urban farmers anywhere and everywhere the couple could think of — Minneapolis, St. Louis, Cincinnati, Chicago, New York City, several parts of California and his hometown of Denver. He hoped the seeds might help alleviate the food shortages and long lines at grocery stores and food banks in economically disadvantaged communities hit hard during the pandemic.

His effort of putting out beets with his beats was a success. And, more than a year later, his seed business is still growing. Vita is among an expanding list of Black gardening enthusiasts-turned-entrepreneurs across the country. They run seed businesses that have benefited from the pandemic-inspired global gardening boom that seed providers, still overwhelmed with orders, hope won't subside anytime soon.

Gods Garden Girl, Coco and Seed, Urban Farms Garden Shop and I Grow Shit are all Black-owned companies that share in Vita's mission of drawing more diverse people into gardening and also illuminating it as an active, pandemic-safe pastime that facilitates healthy eating.
It also provides an escape from stress, including racial stress, which has simmered and exploded at times after George Floyd's murder in Minneapolis.

Research has found that exposure to plants and green spaces while gardening is beneficial to mental and physical health. In fact, a 2018 article in Clinical Medicine noted that merely viewing plants can reduce stress and diminish feelings of fear, anger or sadness by reducing blood pressure and pulse rate and also relieving muscle tension. The same report urged health professionals to encourage their patients to spend time in green spaces and to work in gardens.

Leah Penniman, a farmer and food activist in New York, wrote in her book "Farming While Black" that Black America's connection to seeds dates to the days of enslavement, when some Africans braided seeds into their hair when they were shipped away from home. It was, as Penniman wrote, "insurance for an uncertain future."

But many Black people in the U.S. have intentionally disconnected from farming since then because of its association with the painful legacy of slavery, said Natalie Baszile, author of a recently published anthology on African American farmers and the "Queen Sugar" novel that inspired the Oprah Winfrey Network TV drama centered on a Black family's Louisiana farm.
"Part of our cultural narrative has been to move away from the land, because moving away from the land represents progress," Baszile said. "The farther away you are from the land, the more successful you are. You go away to school, you get your education, you get another degree, you get a job in a field where you don't have your hands in the soil."

But Baszile, too, hopes the seed and gardening trend will inspire more Black people to see the health benefits of gardening. "There is a therapeutic element to being outside planting, even if it's just a flower garden," she said. "There is something absolutely essential and healthy and meditative about getting outside doing something physical; you're moving your body, you are getting exercise, you're breathing clean air, you're connecting to the Earth." And she said connecting to the soil empowers people, whether they are growing their own food or selling seeds as an entrepreneur.

The owner of Melanated Organic Seeds, Devona Stevenson, agrees. She said she initially took up gardening for relaxation in 2018 after a bout of depression. She then launched her seed business last June at the height of the pandemic, because she saw a need, even dating to her days growing up near Miami.

"All I saw around me was fast food and people eating junk food from the corner store," said Stevenson, who is relocating from Fort Lauderdale, Florida, to nearly 2 acres in Fayetteville, Georgia. "I believe that representation matters. So, basically, I saw a need and decided to fill it. For me, it's also about reaching an untapped market, a group of people that have not really been marketed to, in terms of gardening and farming."

Her efforts are not going unnoticed. Stevenson said her list of Instagram followers has swelled from 7,000 to more than 20,000 since she began posting gardening tips last July. She said she believes many Black seed business owners like her are driven by the need for education and economic empowerment.

"My business is for all people — we're all human — but I happen to be a Black woman and a business owner, and if someone out there wants to support a Black-owned business, a Black gardening business, we provide them with that opportunity," she said.

Vita's entrepreneurial endeavor — "pushing seeds," as he calls it — seems to be having an impact, too. Online site Thrillist named him one of its "Heroes of 2020" and Oscar-winning actor Natalie Portman included his "Sprout That Life" line, which runs about $19 for three packs of 55 to 100 seeds each, in her 2020 Top Gift Picks list in the December issue of People magazine. Actor Mark Ruffalo followed by publicly donating money to Vita's GoFundMe campaign that supported his seed distribution effort, prompting social media shoutouts from rapper Cardi B and comedian Cedric the Entertainer.

Vita said he sees the fruits of his efforts in the photos people send to him of the food grown from his seeds. He could not be prouder of how he is reaching communities of color, especially Black communities, who he said disproportionately live in food deserts and are plagued by health disparities. "I wanted to change the way that they're eating, let alone change the economic approach," he said.

To date, with crowdfunding support, he has distributed more than 20,000 of his seed packets free of charge. He said he hopes the effort, along with his online vegan cooking and gardening demonstrations, will help inspire more Black people to try a plant-based diet and spark, well, a growing movement.

"If we can flood our community with unhealthy food and drugs, I believe we can also flood it with seeds and love," he said. "We can flood it with positivity and urban farming and juice bars; without gentrification, without the urban renewal replacement."

KHN (Kaiser Health News) is a national newsroom that produces in-depth journalism about health issues. Together with Policy Analysis and Polling, KHN is one of the three major operating programs at KFF (Kaiser Family Foundation). KFF is an endowed nonprofit organization providing information on health issues to the nation.

"I INSERTED A CHIP IN THE BASE OF YOUR SKULL," THE DOCTOR STATED WITH A PROUD SMILE. "I BELIEVE THAT THIS IS HOW WE CAN BRING YOU BACK TO LIFE AFTER YOUR **EXECUTION.**"

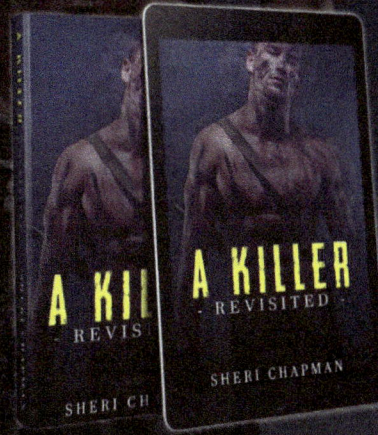

TRIENT PRESS

SHERI CHAPMAN

A KILLER REVISITED

TWO YEARS AGO: *Sylvia Turner's house*

A knock resounded through her house. Sylvia sat at her desk with stacks of research around her. She hopped up and slapped a hand on a stack of papers to keep them from toppling. She peeked out the hole and her jaw clenched. It was her father. She opened the door anyway.

"Hi, Dad," Sylvia sighed. "Come on in."

Mathew Turner entered with several files tucked under his arm.

"What do you have this time?" she asked. Her hand propped on a hip.

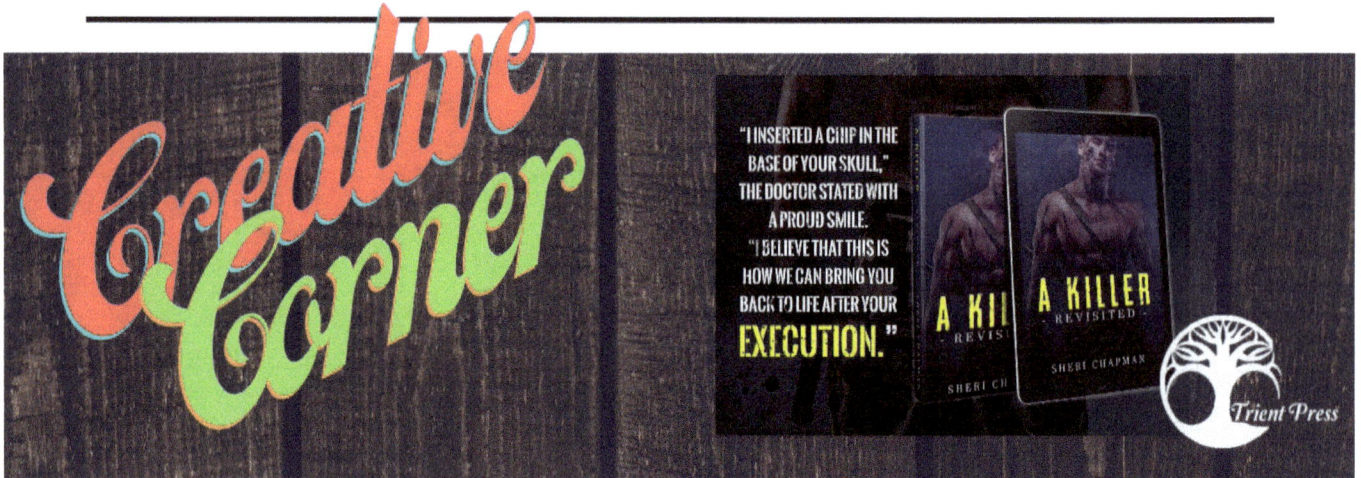

Her father sat on her couch, slightly out of breath. His eyes were vibrant and flashed with excitement.

"Just hear me out, Sylvia. I know your passion is environmental biology, but that's not where the money is."

"Dad, we've talked about this a million times. You do you, and I'll do me."

"I have a great opportunity for you, Dear."

"I don't care, Dad. What you do is unethical. It was kind of okay when people volunteered for your... experiments, but now you're at the prison... what you do isn't right."

Dr. Turner's lips pursed. "Just hear me out."

Sylvia settled on the chair and leaned back. Another soft sigh. "Make it quick. I have work to do." Her eyes flitted to the piles on her desk.

"Sylvia. I love you. You're the only person of meaning in my life. I hate to see you whittle your life away... studying deer or something silly like that. I know you think what I do is unethical, but if you work with me, you'll see how it's the key to the future. I want to share that ride with you."

"Dad. Do people want to participate in your studies? Have you even asked them?"

"That's beside the point."

"No. It isn't. Even prisoners... have rights."

"Hum. Well, we may not see eye-to-eye on every point, but the bigger picture is how we can create a better future." Her father's eyes flashed.

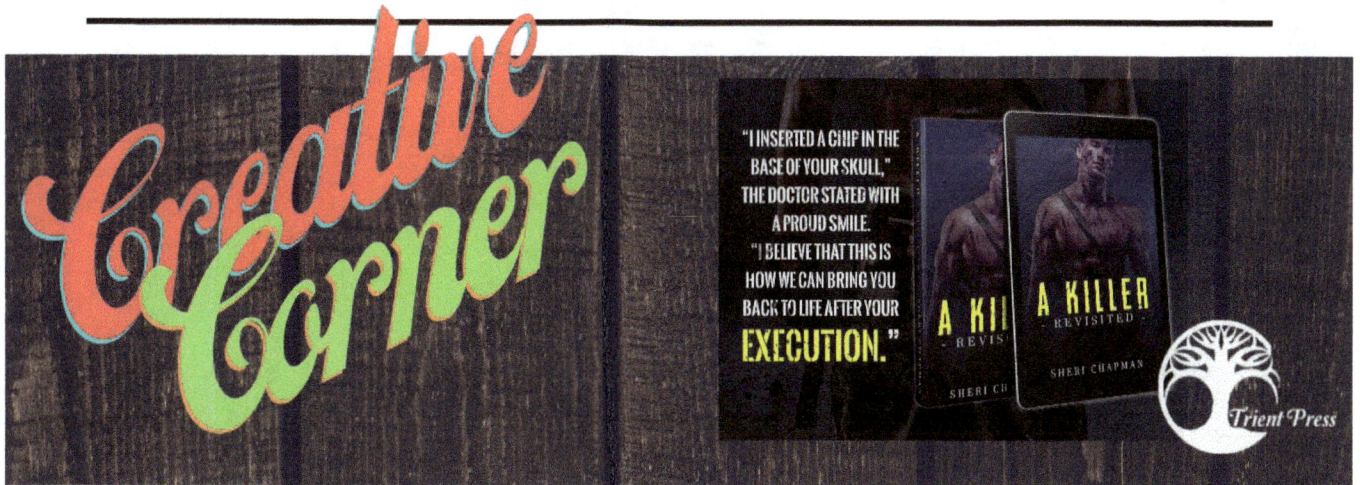

"By sacrificing inmates?" she scoffed. "Better future or not. Your ways are unethical. No future can justify that."

"If you want to study the deer population, you go where the deer are. You try to figure out what's killing them, what food benefits them, and so on. I'm doing the same. I'm studying a population of men who are incarcerated. It's easier to collect data when your subjects are confined to a certain area."

"That's hardly the same, Dad."

"You're right about that. No one cares about the deer population... or wolf... or bird, not really. People will care about what I do, once I'm published. Please, Sylvia. Please, come along with me."

Sylvia intentionally sighed louder. "Dad, I love you, too, but I'm truly tired of talking about this. How 'bout I make us breakfast-for-dinner? I'm going to prove my work is just as important before this is all over with. But first let's eat. No more talk about the future, okay?"

"You bet, Honey. But this isn't over."

Sylvia nodded. "You can turn on the television if you want." She headed for the kitchen.

Dr. Turner flipped on the TV. When his daughter was out of sight, he went to the secret fireproof safe in her closet. He slid a few files inside and put a few winter coats on top. Tomorrow, when she had class, he'd return and move the safe to a more secluded location in her house.

Sheri Chapman loves life and laughing, but you couldn't tell it by her work - from historical romances, suspense, dark fiction, or horror stories. A former teacher of thirty years and mother to four grown daughters, you can follow her on Facebook, Instagram and Twitter to find information and links to her books.

FIND A KILLER REVISITED HERE:
https://www.amazon.com/Killer-Revisited-Sheri-Chapman-ebook/dp/B097QRQ337

DIARY OF AN ONLINE PROFESSOR

By Marilyn Carroll, PhD

Marilyn Carroll

Interview with Dr. Carroll

In a World of Fuzzy Logic

Your book "Diary of an Online Professor" became a reality through that experience?

As a child born to a child in an environment that wasn't necessarily conducive to anyone in my position. The technology we are blessed with today open ups avenues of possibilities for a different delivery of that education so that the instructor's focus is more on those things the instructor needs to focus on where technology then can take all of those things that are labor-intensive that cause the educator not to be able to deliver the most authentic learning experience for students to educate the individual at that individuals need level. Since I came into education 11 years ago from corporate America, it has just shown me so many things that from a business perspective, we could do better by integrating effective tactics which helps to meet education at student-centered levels. By doing so it is my belief that we deliver better results and outcomes for all stakeholders, i.e., students, teachers, administrators, communities, etc.

Would you mind telling us a little about what you do?

I am a businesswoman, writer, college business professor, training and development professional, researcher, mother of a college student, grandmother of a child in elementary school, and a college student myself. I am the picture of the individual in search and need of education that speaks to me and my needs and goals. Basically, I am a busy person with competing priorities but a lifelong learner who values education.

Where did the idea for the book come from?

In the midst of writing my book on Spiritual Boot Camp, the pandemic occurred. There were so many meetings on education and how education was going to be delivered to students. In addition, I was working on a proposal from my business on how to deliver diversity, equity, and inclusion training to Dallas ISD starting July 2020. Virtually was my answer to the proposal, and I develop how to make it effective, engaging, and efficient. And I had to put that in a bid proposal. In addition, I was pretty successful at delivering online education to my students and my clients that came to my virtual seminars. I felt that I had a winning combination that was the secret sauce, so I decided to use my daily diary entries on my experience as an online professor and educator, and training professional to document that evidence of the secret sauce.

Why do adults and children alike enjoy your classes?

My relatability quotient. I deliver learning content in a way that is relatable where my audience no matter their age group, race or ethnicity understands it. My secret sauce to teaching is to make it engaging, interactive, and to package the educational experience for students with knowledge and wisdom, but make it entertaining. The secret sauce has several ingredients:
1. Entertaining,
2. Educational,
3. an unforgettable experience
4. Make it applicable to real-life scenarios
5. Fill it with inspirational messages of hope, gratitude, and resilience

The Sauce combined with the approach make for outcomes for students, learners and organizations that shown to provide 80-90 percent engagement and completion outcomes while building critical thinking and communication skills.

How can our readers find you?
They can email me Marilyn@drmarilyncarroll.com or marilyn@carrollbeck.com or they can call me at 214.301.1664.

To read the full interview, please visit us at: https://trientpressmagazine.com/

DRESSING MISS
DAISY

PURA VIDA

LIVE FREE

FLOWER STYLES

WHO DOESN'T LOVE A FRESH PICKED FLORAL STACK?

BREAK THE SILENCE. BREAK THE CHAINS.
HELP
STOP
HUMAN
TRAFFICKING
Join the fight at humantraffickinghotline.org

LAYERS REVEALED

BY: KRISTINA WENZL-FIGUEROA

I have been blessed with a couple of weeks to enjoy my kids and although there's always work, I've made the choice to take this time to not only work on breathing and slowing down a bit, but also to dig deeper into who I am. To peel back the layers.

I think that many of us move at such a fast pace that we lose sight of who we are. We become the titles that we assume and the roles that we play in other's lives. I reduce myself to only Chief Operating Officer of Trient Press, Partner and Owner of ZenTerra Waterscapes, that Novelist, busy Screenwriter, my husband's wife, my children's mother... and although we most certainly know who we once were, maybe even who we were before this latest season in our lives, we grow, evolve and CHANGE.

I have changed.

I've been really asking the questions that we never honestly ask: Who am I? What do I truly find fulfilling? Do I like the person I've become? Do I like where I'm headed? Is what I'm giving out in my career, life, friendships, balanced by what I get back in return? Am I trying my hardest at life or just half-assing it?

These are the deep questions that take more than a moment to know the answer. They take deep reflection and then the willingness to analyze the intuitive answers that we're given. Some of us pray, several of us meditate, many of us journal and a few of us are able to look inward and feel the answers—but all of these techniques get us closer to US. The Us that we keep guarded and protected from most people in our lives.

I think the reason that we don't always truly show others who we are, is because it makes us too vulnerable. That —and it's scary to say—but there's a good number of us who don't know who we are any better than the people around us know us.

To really get to know ourselves we must spend time alone with ourselves... and this doesn't mean with a latte or glass of wine in front of the TV. It means genuinely getting to know who we are deep inside. Asking the important questions and then listening to our hearts for the answers.

This process is...
UNCOMFORTABLE.

66 *Once you do the work, it is so worth it.*

This process may be TIME CONSUMING. This process is most certainly EXHAUSTING... but you know what? Once you do the work it is so worth it because YOU actually become YOU and not a robot version of yourself going through the motions. You become a more authentic version of yourself and begin the first step to living a better life.

"So, now what?" you ask. You have done the work; you've peeled back the onion layers and you are not thrilled with what you're doing or where you're at. Maybe you aren't even passionate about where you're heading...

So, what can you do?

Have courage first of all. It takes a lot of bravery to look at yourself and your life and really think about if it makes you happy. Not everyone can or is willing to do the work, so congratulate yourself and then take a deep breath.

Start making changes.

If there are toxic people in your life, begin to distance yourself. If you have unhealthy vices, quit them. I suggest—and I'm not a doctor, but this is what has worked for me—stop cold turkey. If you are tempted to stop at a bakery, find a different route home. If where you socialize after work includes smoking and drinking... find a different hangout. If your job isn't fulfilling, start looking at ways that bring fulfillment into your career. I know this isn't always possible, but rest assured even small things can create ripples that make bigger ripples that eventually might get you to that next step of fulfillment.

Changes can also just be about you.

Change your narrative. This means change the conversations that you have with yourself in your head. Talk to yourself differently—if you're telling yourself how shitty the world is, then will you ever see its beauty?

Be thankful for the small things. There's ALWAYS something to be thankful for. Start by writing down things that you are thankful for. It is surprisingly harder after you get down the big things but treat it as part of your daily routine. Make time to find thanks for the little stuff.

Invest in yourself. Purchase a few new wardrobe pieces or that new make-up you've been wanting. Start eating healthier or join that gym that you've been putting off because you just didn't have the time. If you begin to change how you see yourself on the outside, how you see yourself from the inside will also change.

Peeling back the layers is hard work—and anyone who says differently is either truly gifted or didn't do the work. I have found in the last few weeks that once you begin to change the world you live in, then how you view your world will also change.
So, I encourage you to make a date with yourself and get to know the true you.

Kristina Wenzl-Figueroa is a full-time business owner, entrepreneur, and homeschooling stay-at-home mom. She loves to write and has several contemporary and adult romances under the pen name, Tina Maurine. You can like and follow her on Facebook, Instagram and Twitter under her pen name or visit her website for more information on her books.
https://tinamaurine.com/

CHANGE ONLY HAPPENS WHEN YOU STEP OUT OF YOUR COMFORT ZONE
AND ONTO A NEW PATHWAY.

WWW.JGMACINDOE.COM

POSSIBILITIES ARE ENDLESS, AND THE OPPORTUNITIES ARE BOUNDLESS
WHEN YOU ALLOW YOURSELF TO BELIEVE YOU CAN ACHIEVE ANYTHING
YOU PUT YOUR MIND TO IT.

I WILL ASSIST YOU IN YOUR JOURNEY OF SECURING DIGITAL BUSINESS
OWNERSHIP.

WHAT YOU WILL LEARN

- How to build a foudation for a successful business
- Strategies to automate your business
- Where to get business coaching/ mentoring

ABOUT OUR CULTURE

Imagine the advantage you would gain by plugging into a global community of like-minded digital entrepreneurs.

M.I. Ruscsak

The Art of Influencer Marketing

What is it, and how to connect with the right influencers.

As explained by a social media influencer and business owner.

As both authors or entrepreneurs, we all hear about social media influencers in the way for products to be found. This sounds like a great slogan right: "Social media influencers leading the way replacing the ads of yesterday." But what is influencer marketing anyways? How do you do it? How do you find influencers that suit your business? Or better question, what businesses can profit from finding influencers?

The short answer is really simple, every business can benefit from social media influencers. And when I mean any business, I mean any media, B2B companies, authors and direct to consumer. Any and all businesses if done properly can benefit. However, this is a theory because you have to know what you're looking for and how to connect. Influencer marketing requires

research. It requires actively finding the influencers that are tailored for your company. Sure, there are some that are very diversified, and when I say diversified I actually mean they do not hold themselves to one niche. These are the influencers who like to help other products besides just one thing. They are the ones that will do hair, makeup, beauty, fashion, and business music. They don't tie themselves down to just one thing. These are the ones that are more authentic; they represent real life. At the same time you still have to do your research. You do not want to go to an influencer who only does hair and makeup and you are in real estate.

Sure, the hair and makeup influencer might have two million followers but of those two million followers how many are actually in the market for a new house? I know what you're thinking in the market of two million followers even if 10% look at the ad for this new housing development, that's still enough people to buy your product, or is it? You have to look at the 10% to see where they are and if they're even in the same area where your research is being made, a lot of social media influencers such as myself have followers across the globe. This seems like a daunting task. Lots of research for something that should be simple but it works.

Now for an author, social media influencers are a little bit different, or are only different if we're not utilizing the full power of social media. Authors tend to be beta readers. Now, what is a beta reader compared to a social media influencer? Beta readers get a product- in this case a book- leave a review on places such as Amazon. This is all they do. Let's go one step further. Social media influencers, depending on the type of influence you get, will not only leave a review on places like Amazon but will also promote your product to their following.

Stop, read that last sentence again.

A social media influencer will read your book, review your product and promote it to their following. I know some of you might say, well beta readers are free. But are they? A beta reader gets a free copy of your book in most cases an ebook. So they are getting a free product. They are bartering their time to give you a review on a single website. How many hours does it take for them to review one book, write the review on one website and will they promote that book to their following? If no one knows about the book because no one is promoting the book, what good is that one review?

Okay, so we understand a beta reader is an old school influencer. New school influencers are your social media influencers. Let's change the game now. Does this mean authors know how to find beta readers who are actually social media influencers? Does this mean other businesses know how to find social media influencers for their products? Ladies and gentlemen, you are all entrepreneurs. You are all business professionals. It does not matter if I speak to you as an entrepreneur, if I speak to you as an author, you are one in the same. Every product regardless of if it is a book, a new face cream, or new piece of tech, can benefit from social media influencers if you know where to find them.

So, let me help you with a few sites that I know that you can join to find the social media influencers that your company needs.

https://Influencers.findyourinfluence.com
https://afluencer.com/
https://intellifluence.com/

Now, once you sign up for one of these sites your work truly begins as there are few different types of social media influencers. As with any site regardless if you pay for it or it's free you have to build your portfolio. Your business profile. What kind of social media influencer are you looking for? How much are you willing to pay them for their time in marketing? Now let's be honest, some will barter with you. I mean after all, everyone loves free items.

In the case of books, these can be your ebooks; they do not need to be physical copies; however, if you give away a physical copy of your book then the social media influencer can hold the product in the ad that they were placing on to their social media platform. This exactly is the same if it's eyeliner, lipstick, face cream, piece of tech... whatever it is. If you give away the item to the social media influencer for free and you put it in there they must include the picture of the item in the post, now they are not just talking about it but they were being seen with it.

Then you have the other social media influencers that expect to be paid something for their time on top of the free item. There's various ways that they come up with how much their time is worth to post your item onto their social media page. If you're using one of the sites listed either you can't see if the influencer is someone that expects to be paid, or barter, or both. If they are looking for payment, many will put in their bio with the minimum that they were except this can be as low as $5; however, it can go up to $700 and above if the social media influencer has more than 70,000 followers.

Okay, fine. I get it you're looking for free marketing because your company cannot afford to pay someone for reviews or for placing something on social media. I get it.

But what does *free* really mean?

Okay, so you're going to go on to say Instagram looks for social media influencers that have between 5,000 and 70,000 followers. Write a pitch for them that is tailored to your product. Offer them a discount on the item or a free item- yet they still have to cover the shipping and handling fee. Okay, so this takes you all of 15 minutes to write one pitch. Now, do this a hundred times. What is your time worth? Is it worth you doing all the legwork post in the pitch to

100 different social media influencers? If they want the physical product, then you have to still ship the product to them and pay the shipping and handling cost unless digital. Then, you must still communicate with them after. Or, do you create a profile to five different influencer sites and let the influencers come to you?

As a business owner, I can tell you time is money. My time is precious and I do not have time to reach out to hundreds of influencers about my products. However, I do have time to post a single ad on one of these sites that hire influencers and let the influencers come to me. It takes a lot less time for me to answer an email or message on one of these sites than it does to reach a hundred influencers on just Instagram. This is my choice. This is a choice that I use to run my business in marketing.

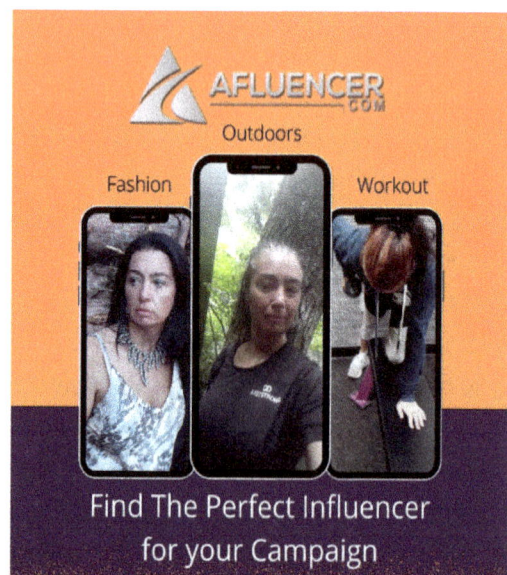

Victorious PR

🌐 https://victoriouspr.com/

✉ support@victoriouspr.com

📞 (702) 718- 5821

Don't take our word for it

"Literal GOLD. If your clients don't know you, they aren't going to trust you and Victoria has helped me overcome that and so much more. She got me on Yahoo! Finance and it absolutely blew my mind! I've been over the moon with the quality of work."

Bao Le | CEO of Bao Digital

Real Estate:
Praise from the
Real Estate Industry

Victoria did amazing things. Uncovered things that I never even thought of like going to different publications and getting us sent to those publications, with stories and was able to get us sent to the RJ and which is a huge local newspaper. And I got a lot of personal private messages. She uncovered a lot of ways to get our brand and my face out in front of people that I would have never imagined I could have been in front of.

Coltyn Simmons Founder of Custom Fit Real Estate

Praise from the
Entrepreneurs Industry

"You've done a great job, Victoria. Thank you so much. All these articles were wonderful and I love having the logos behind my name now it just gives us more credibility."

Krista Mashore Coach, Best Selling Author

FEATURED IN:

inman Forbes Entrepreneur yahoo! finance

abc TODAY GSD FOX NEWS

📷 thevictoriakennedy f @thevictoriouspr 🐦 @GoVictoriaK in victoriajkennedy

VICTORIOUS PR

What We Do

We create Industry Leaders
We help businesses be seen as the #1 Authority in their niche.

Your next giant leap leans on more than metrics, channels, and platforms alone. It requires a pitch-perfect mix of strategic precision, deeply human thinking, creative prowess, and some love.

Victorious PR is a global agency working across fields to build brands that attract, brands that offer a unique position, and brands that effect real change in the world.

REAL ESTATE

Although the real estate mantra is "location, location, location," we're all about "public relations, public relations, public relations." What good is a great loaction's availablity, if no one knows about it?

ENTREPRENEURS

No matter what stage of business you're in, know that your story matters. We put you in the forefrount to get the right notoeriety you deserve.

AND SO MUCH MORE...

One Of Our Success Stories

While most people can't handle one job, Farrah Ali has three. During the day she is a fulltime insurance professional, at night she is a full time investor and she is the author of Diaries of a Female Real Estate Investor. To top it all off, the most important job for her is being a single mother to her two kids.

Farrah has been a crucial piece to the growth of Chicago REIA since the beginning. Her journey with investing started in June of 2014, now just four short years later she is at twenty-five rental properties, one flip, and eight wholesale deals.

Farrah Ali
REAL ESTATE INVESTOR
ENTREPRENEUR & AUTHOR

FARRAH ALI

Real Estate Investor, Entrepreneur & Author
www.farrahali.org

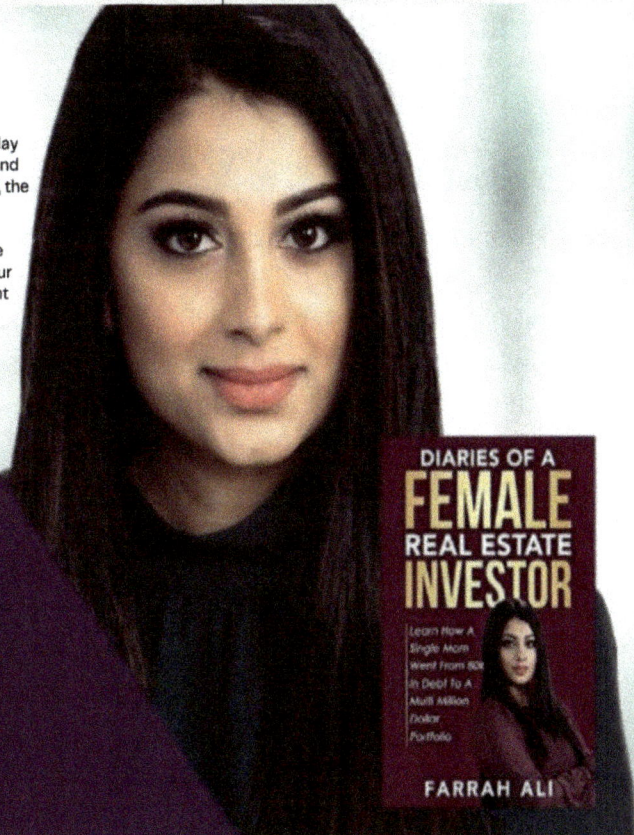

DIARIES OF A FEMALE REAL ESTATE INVESTOR

Learn How A Single Mom Went From 80k In Debt To A Multi Million Dolar Portfolio

FARRAH ALI

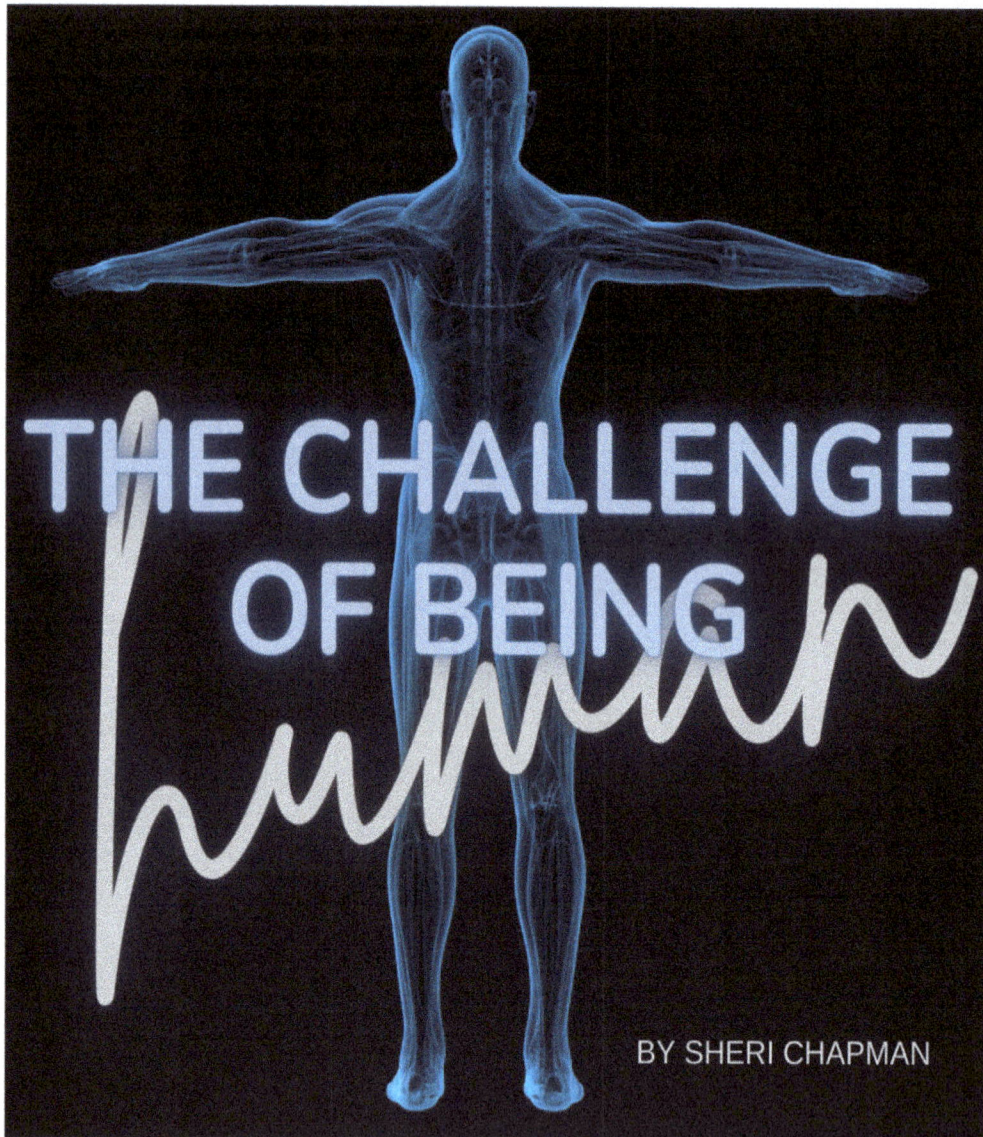

THE CHALLENGE OF BEING human

BY SHERI CHAPMAN

Being human means overcoming fear and growing into your potential. Life is full of choices.

But really, do we have a choice? Life is all about change and growth. But… what if we don't want to grow and change? We can postpone the inevitable and choose not to grow… but it's always lurking in the corner, encouraging you to make that decision.

In my point of view, these are our options:

- Do we sink down, spiraling out of control and regress until we hit rock bottom before we choose something different? If not, how many times are we willing to keep hitting that miserable wall?
- Do we stagnate and wait for a catalyst to shake us to our core before we move forward?
- Or do we grab the bull by the horns and manifest our "destiny" with abundance and love?

The choice seems obvious. Why, then, do so many of us choose to be complacent?

Fear. Fear of change is scarier than our current situation, even if that happens to be horrible. If we like the way our life is going, even though it could be better, why should we *want* to change? The unknown *could be worse* than the present circumstances. It could be better, of course, but fear is that deterrent.

I am one of the guilty as charged.

I strive to move forward and be an agent of change, but I have my own demons to face.

Again, the human experience makes us question ourselves.

- Am I worthy?
- Am I smart enough?
- Am I innovative enough?
- Is my knowledge enough that I'll be valued?

I've decided to change my views of myself, too. I know that I'm good at everything I've had time to learn and practice, but on new endeavors, I have shaky confidence. I don't know what I'm doing, and I'm afraid I will look "less than" others who may have had more experience or knowledge on the subject. You guessed it: Fear of Failure. But in reality, who doesn't experience

this? It can be applied to any job.

Mother. Wife. Author. Teacher. Nurturer. Exercise instructor. Mentor. Friend. Advocate. Animal lover. Entrepreneur. Bowler. Runner. Scuba diver. The list goes on.

Have I succeeded at each? **Yes.**
Have I failed at each? **Yes.**

The difference is… do you have the COURAGE to get up and try again?

I've made up my mind to have a **personal mantra** –my affirmation– if you will. It is simply this: I am smart. I am confident. I am valuable, and I am worthy. I love to learn, and I have skill.

Support is very valuable. Fear and judgment can be overcome. Just remember, self love is vital, and with it, anything is possible.

Sheri Chapman loves life and laughing, but you couldn't tell it by her work - from historical romances, suspense, dark fiction, or horror stories. A former teacher of thirty years and mother to four grown daughters, you can follow her on Facebook, Instagram and Twitter to find links to her books.

ROCK YOUR AUDIENCE!

with Rocky Romanella

SUCCESS - WHAT DOES THAT WORD MEAN TO YOU?

During a recent interview which has been published in Street Insider, Market Minute on ABC News and NBC News Digital, and International Business Times we discussed a wide range of topics. You can read the entire interview on our web site at https://www.3sixtymanagementservices.com/category/interviews/.

Here is one of the questions we discussed: *Speaking of success, what does the word mean to you?*

In my view, successful leadership is about building a bridge to the future. You give your people the opportunity to help build that bridge by communicating and educating each one of them on your vision and strategy.

Successful leaders can quickly, accurately, and effectively assess:

- Who they are.
- What they stand for.
- What they will never compromise.

More importantly these leaders are always checking and verifying, does this match their vision and strategy, and does it correspond to what your people, your customers and investors believe to be your strategy, and consistently reflect the brand.

Success is always leaving things a little better than you found them. Customers are better because of the interaction with your company, people are better because of the time they are with you, and shareowners and stakeholder are better because of your stewardship and leadership.

In summary the successful leader is the person who adds value as a trusted advisor, mentor and visionary who uses a process approach to lead the organization. A process approach allows your success to be consistent and enduring. It will elevate your people to new levels of success. Great organizations need to have a thoughtful vision and strategy. Great leaders need to combine that strategic vision with the ability to tactically execute the strategy.

For the rest of the story and this interview visit: https://www.3sixtymanagementservices.com/category/interviews/.

For more on leadership and many other topics, pick up your copy of TIGHTEN THE LUG NUTS and visit our website at: http://www.tightenthelugnuts.com.

Feel free to visit our newsletter section at: https://www.3sixtymanagementservices.com/category/newsletters/
.

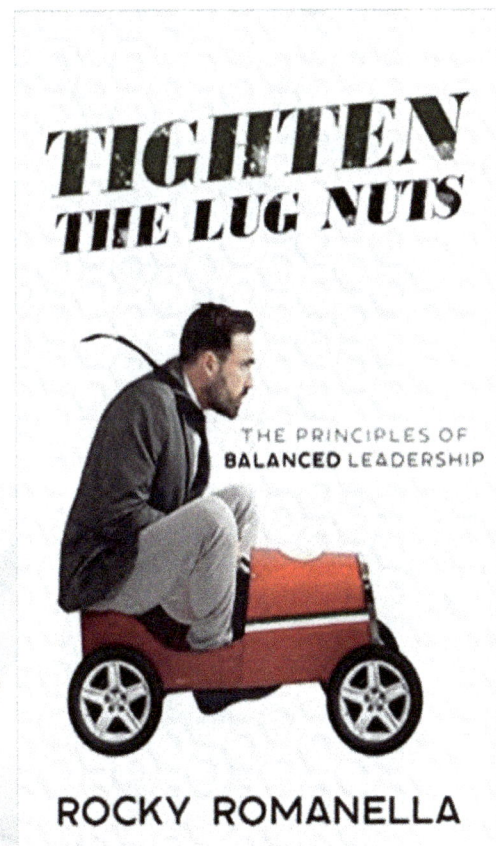

Lessons from the book

Tighten The Lug Nuts

TIGHTEN THE LUG NUTS

THE PRINCIPLES OF **BALANCED** LEADERSHIP

ROCKY ROMANELLA

TightenTheLugNuts.com

ADVICE

BY: HOLLY K

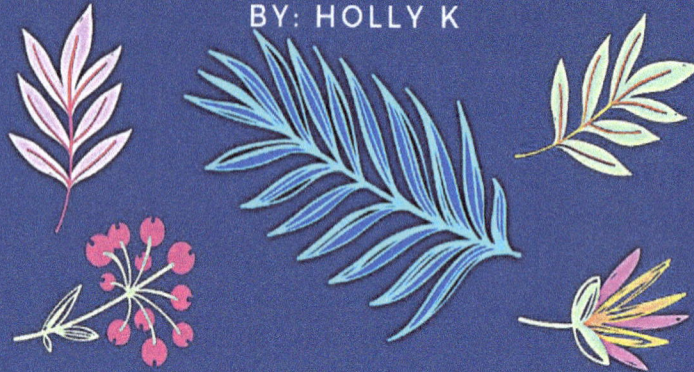

WELL BEING

By: HOLLY K BROOKS

Intuitive Life Coach & Psychic Reader In The United States

One-On-One Readings & Spiritual Life Coaching

If you are wrestling with a challenge that needs an answer, please send your questions to Trient Press Magazine.....

ADVICE

Dear Holly K,

I'm writing to you because I am completely confused. Admittedly, things were difficult at home with my kids and my husband during quarantine; however, as we slowly morph into the "new normal" things are a mess. First, my husband is working from home. He is noisy, talks very loud on the phone, and it disrupts the entire house. If I ask him to close the office door, he says ok and then he does not. My children, ages 10, 7, and 4, are home because it is summer vacation. The entire last 14 months have been summer vacation meaning they have been home, virtual learning. They are fighting with each other, are always saying they are bored, and frankly I can't keep them busy enough. As for me, I am not sure I even have a life of my own anymore. All my energy is spent dealing with everyone else and making sure they're ok. Holly K, I want my own life, I want my children to be happy, and something must be done about my husband's work. Please advise me.

Signed,

Covid Hungover.

ADVICE

Dear Ms.. Hungover,

First, you are not alone. Everybody is feeling the same pressures and having the same problems you are. Covid-19 affected us socially, emotionally, and has tested our personal strength. As far as your husband is concerned - BOUNDARIES. Sit down with him and tell him what you told me. He needs to understand that the energy in your house has been disrupted. He can help to bring back peace and stability by working in a room where he closes his door and separates his work from the house. As far as the children go, their lack of socialization, not being able to go into their school and see their friends has been extremely difficult and their emotions are all wrapped up in a big knot. Try to keep them busy as possible; sports, arts and crafts, dancing, gymnastics, games, and reading books, to name a few. Now, to the most important person, you are the glue for everything. You need to install BOUNDARIES as well or you will get lost in the sauce. Carve out some alone time, make it happen. Without you, none of this is possible. Go get your nails done, go for a walk by yourself, spend some time with other moms. I totally understand your predicament, there is a way to mitigate all of this. My money's on you.

New Normal?

Holly K

ADVICE

Dear Holly K,
I just found out that my husband of 20 years has been selling "feet pictures" online. I am weirded out! What would possess him to do this? After 20 years naturally, there is not much spice left in our sex life. I am trying to understand. I would love to hear your thoughts on this. Am I overreacting or should I leave it alone?

Signed,

Are feet sexy?

Dear Sexy Feet,

It sounds to me like your husband has a foot fetish. Sometimes, when things become a little stagnant in your sex life; it follows that he would look to something else to excite him sexually. I do not know about you, but I would prefer a man that had a foot fetish rather than having affairs with other women. If it is not taking up too much of his time, let it go. A few harmless online pictures of various feet are a lot less threatening to your marriage than other sexual scenarios. You are not overreacting; it is in fact surprising and a cause for a lot of questions. I suggest that you take pictures of your own feet in different poses and send them to him. This way, you have got some skin in the game, so be creative! Signed,

Fetishes are OK,

Holly K

ADVICE

Dear Maybe Ménage a Trois,

Dear Holly K,

My wife has this new friend. I happen to like her and I'm glad that she has found a good friend. They seem to be hanging out together more and more, lately. At first it did not mean that much to me, but I think that something might be going on between them. If my wife is happy with this situation, should I ignore it or join in? I find the whole idea of joining in rather exciting. I am at a loss though as how to approach her.

Signed,

Ménage a?

These days being polyamorous is becoming more and more acceptable. New variations on sexual experiences between married couples are morphing and changing. Sometimes marriage does not mean that you are sexually tied forever. If your wife is exploring new sexual possibilities, obviously she is searching for something that she feels is lacking. Possibly, this new "relationship" is because she needs something more. You can relax, it is not a threat to your marriage. As far as you joining in, fling yourself into the whole situation. Sit down with your wife and her friend and discuss how to proceed. All three of you need to be on the same page with the same parameters. Remove all pre-programmed emotions, e.g., guilt, shame, and jealousy. Have an open mind and enjoy yourselves. The worst thing that can happen is that it only happens once.

Signed,

Polyfidelity is OK,

Holly K

Beat the Heat!

Not Your Momma's Margarita.

By: Kristina Figueroa
Photo: iStock

*I love a cool, refreshing beverage that is easy to drink in the heat.
We just made these for my mom's birthday and they were a fabulous hit!*

INGREDIENTS (SINGLE SIZE):

2 OZ. TEQUILA
(We like Hornitos Resposado)

3.5 OZ. MARGARITA MIX
(Baja Bobs is a good sugar free option, but we also like Costco's Kirkland brand)

JUICE FROM 1/4 FRESH LIME

ZEST FROM 1/4 FRESH LIME

(SPLASH OF ICE WATER IF THE MIXER IS TOO SWEET FOR YOUR LIKING)

DIP MOUTH OF THE GLASS IN FRESH LIME JUICE THEN AGAIN IN A BOWL OF RAW SUGAR TO COAT THE BRIM.
POUR YOUR INGREDIENTS OVER ICE AND GIVE IT A QUICK STIR. GARNISH WITH A WEDGE OF FRESH LIME.

Enjoy!

Easy Dinner on a Hot Summer Night!

Fresh Garden-Tomato & Basil Salad

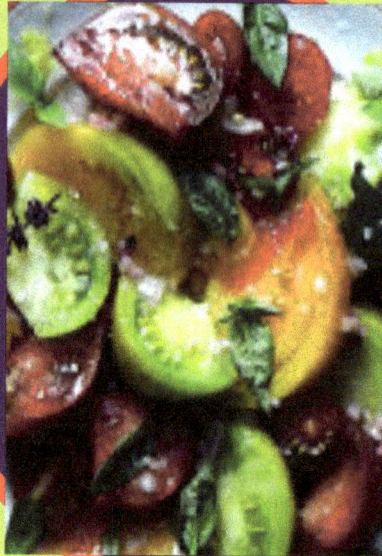

INGREDIENTS:

4-6 MEDIUM- LARGE RIPE HEIRLOOM TOMATOES OR 18-24 CHERRY TOMATOES

6-8 FRESH BASIL LEAVES

EVOO
(EXTRA VIRGIN OLIVE OIL WITH GARLIC IS ALSO A GOOD OPTION.)

BASALMIC VINEGAR
(I PREFER A FIG BASALMIC VINEGAR BUT ANY AGED BASALMIC IS GOOD.)

OPTIONAL INGREDIENTS:

ONION
CUCUMBER OR ZUCHINI
MOZZARELLA
SALT & PEPPER

WASH AND DRY ALL GARDEN VEGETABLES AND HERBS. SLICE TOMATOES INTO BITE-SIZED CHUNKS AND TEAR BASIL.CHOP OPTIONAL INGREDIENTS (I LIKE CUBED FRESH ZUCHINI) INTO ATTRACTIVE CONSISTENT CHUNKS. TOSS WITH A **LIGHT** DRIZZLE OF EVOO OR IT WILL BE TOO OILY AND A MODERATE DRIZZLE OF BASALMIC VINEGAR. SEASON TO TASTE AND TOSS. GARNISH WITH FRESH BASIL.

BY: KRISTINA FIGUEROA
PHOTO: PIXBY

RESOURCES FOR ENTREPRENEURS

How to Create the Best Content Marketing Strategy for Your Niche

Develop a Target Audience With Specific Needs

Research is an essential part of content creation. With millions of blog posts published each day, brands need to find ways to stand out and provide real value to the audiences that they are trying to reach. Each piece of content needs a clear target audience and a need that should be filled. Not only will this make your content more valuable, but it will also help you better come up with ideas for what content to create and when.

Consider the various options available to you for content research. You can learn about your target audience in Google Analytics and use search terms and keyword research to identify their pain points. Some brands go so far as to create charts with audiences, keywords, and then ideas underneath that address their problems. After all, if your content isn't creating value, then why are you spending time on it?

Develop Supporting Content for Your Message

The high-quality content that you create for your audience is known as "cornerstone content." This is content that is valuable, in-depth, and draws people to your page. Cornerstone content may be pages that already rank well (that you want to give a boost to) or new content that you want to promote. The next step in your content marketing strategy is to create supporting content that boosts these cornerstone pieces.

Your supporting content comes in many forms. A few examples include social media posts that drive traffic to your pages, guest posts that feature the highlights of your cornerstone content and link to it, and supplemental blog posts that direct readers to the initial content. As you can see with this process, content marketing promotions require a long-term strategy. You're not just creating content and hoping your audience finds it.

RESOURCES FOR ENTREPRENEURS

Partner With Other Bloggers to Spread Your Message

One strategy you can use to support your content marketing efforts is influencer marketing. This occurs when you partner with various social media accounts and blogs in your industry to point their audiences to your cornerstone content. While you may only have a reach of a thousand or so people, influencers can reach tens of thousands (if not hundreds of thousands) of internet users. You can get your brand in front of new audiences and turn them into fans of what you have to say.

The easiest way to work with influencers is through a service like Intellifluence. You can easily vet people by their niche, audience size, and requirements for content. This way you can find the right influencers to reach your goals. You can also quickly form agreements with what these influencers should post and how they will be compensated for their efforts.

With the right bloggers, you can drive hundreds of people to your cornerstone content who will find value in the posts that you created.

Track Which Content Strategies Worked

Content creation is a cyclical process. You create content, you promote content, and you evaluate how your efforts worked out. If you don't stop to evaluate your work in this last step, you could end up creating content that doesn't appeal to your audience or doesn't drive the results that you want.

Make a note of what content your audience likes and try to replicate that success with similar formats. You may also need to expand upon ideas and develop additional pieces based on audience feedback. For example, if you develop a guide for setting up a pop-up shop, the next logical step could be turning a pop-up shop into a long-term business. This evaluation process can kick off the research for your next piece of cornerstone content so you can identify the target audience and problems that you need to solve.

Creating the right content is essential to connect with your target audience; however, without the right promotions, your hard work and great ideas will never get noticed. By taking a high-level view of your content marketing strategy, you can make sure your pieces provide a real ROI for your brand and help you grow.

Influencers

Every Entrepreneur Know these sites

Upfluence - Find Influencers
https://get.upfluence.com/

**Find & Recruit Influencers - GRIN -
Influencer Marketing**
https://grin.co/

AspireIQ (formerly Revfluence)
https://www.aspireiq.com/

**HypeAuditor - Top Instagram
Influencers Ranking**
https://hypeauditor.com/

Post for Rent
https://www.postforrent.com/

AFLUENCER.COM

Dovetale
https://dovetale.com/

Influence.co
https://Influence.co

collabstr
https://collabstr.com/

socialseo
https://www.socialseo.com/

sproutsocial
https://sproutsocial.com/

**Heepsy | Find influencers
worldwide**
https://www.heepsy.com/

awario
https://awario.com/

Klear
https://klear.com/

Traackr
https://www.traackr.com/

Afluencer
https://afluencer.com/

Intellifluence
Trusted
BLOGGER

LINQIA
Influencer

JUDE
Ouvrard

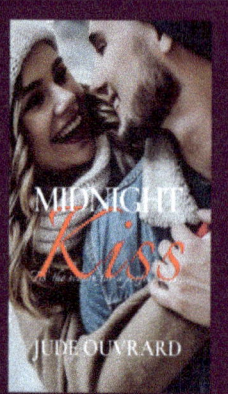

Trient Press

Romance that makes your heart flutter.

Trientrepreneur

A Trient Press Magazine for Authors & Entrepreneurs

The Fallen

From Trient Press

Foreign Languages

Coming Soon

English
German
Dutch
Italian
Spanish
French
Norwegian
Hungarian
Scotts Gaelic
Irish

E-Book
& Paperback

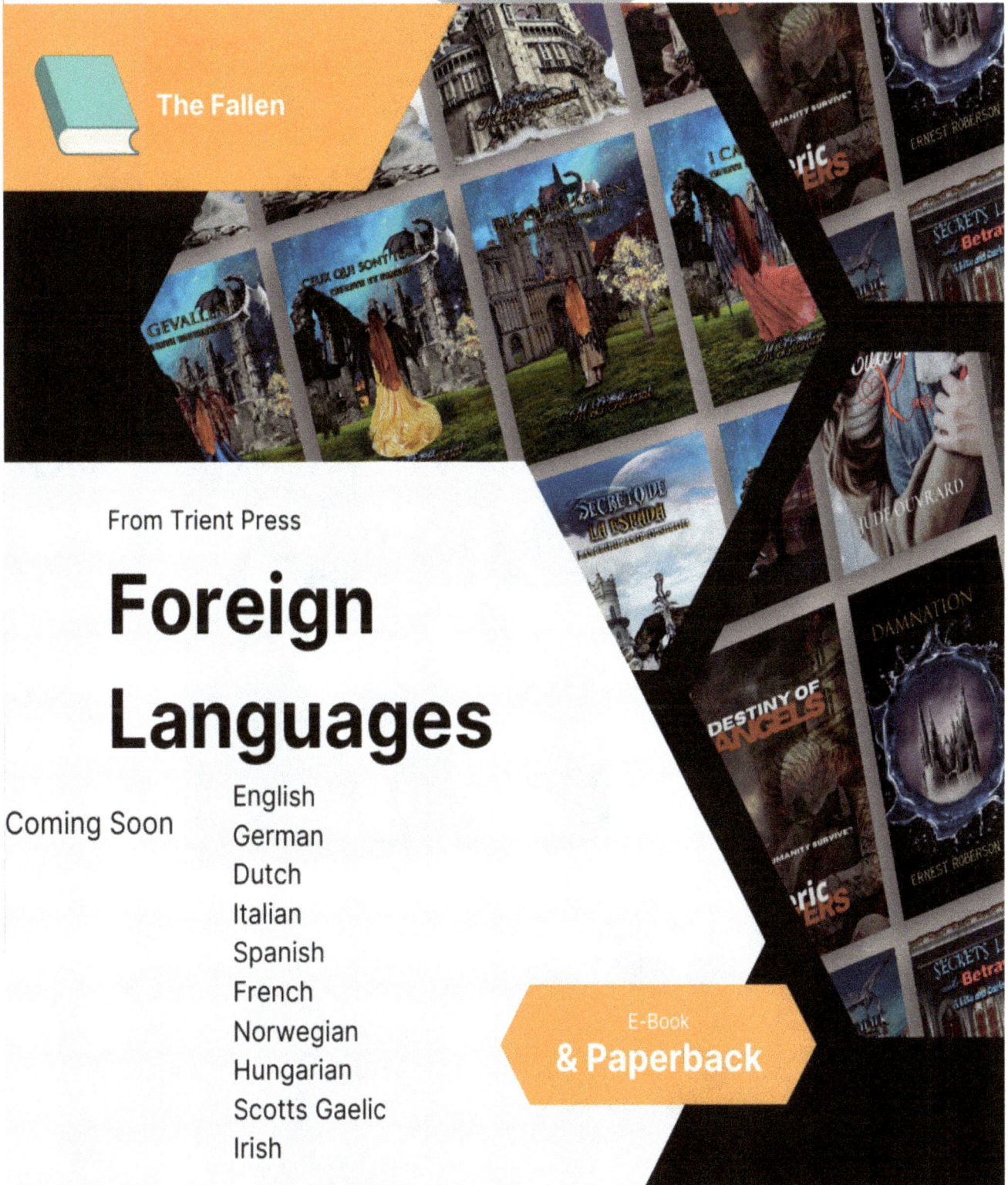

TRIENT PRESS

Magazine

Trientrepreneur

A Trient Press Publication for Authors & Entrepreneurs

Issue 4 | July 2021 $10.99

FEATURED

Former Special Agent, Author Link

ARTICLES

Four Time Management Tactics for Busy Entrepreneurs

How Minimalism Can Help to Clean and Strengthen the Mind

TIPS

Must have information for both authors and entrepreneurs

GUEST ARTICLES

Have something to share with Authors and Entrepreneurs submit a story to: info@trientmagaize.com

INTERVIEWS

For radio interviews there is a fee: https://calendly.com/mlruscsak-ceo/30min

For free printed interviews Contact Info@trientpress.com